10.50

SECULARIZED EUROPE

GOSPEL AND CULTURES PAMPHLET 6

SECULARIZED EUROPE

Who Will Carry Off Its Soul?

Antonie Wessels

WCC Publications, Geneva

Cover design: Edwin Hassink
Cover photo: A hammer of St Martin of Tours (d. 397), who is said to have destroyed pagan temples and built churches and monasteries on the sites. The Latin inscription reads: "The idols fall down, struck by Martin's axe. Let no one believe that those who fall so easily are gods." (Stone ca. 1000 BC, other parts ca. 1300. Museum Catharijneconvent, Utrecht, Netherlands, inventory No. OKM m38)

ISBN 2-8254-1182-5

© 1996 WCC Publications, World Council of Churches,
150 route de Ferney, 1211 Geneva 2, Switzerland

No. 6 in the Gospel and Cultures series

Printed in Switzerland

Table of Contents

ix   INTRODUCTION

1   1. CHRISTIANIZATION, SECULARIZATION AND EUROPEAN CULTURE

8   2. APPROPRIATING THE SACRED

21   3. THE GOSPEL AND CONTEMPORARY EUROPEAN CULTURE

For Miep Uitdenboogaard-de Bel,
who sees with the heart

It is all a parable of a mystery beyond this world.
— Jan Wit

Introduction

According to Greek mythology, Zeus, the chief of the gods, kidnapped Europa, the daughter of the king of Phoenicia. He did so by approaching her in the shape of a bull. When she sat upon the beautiful bull, it took her to Crete, where Zeus revealed himself to her in his true form.

The ancient Greek story of Europa is one of the myths recounted in the *Metamorphoses* of the Latin poet Ovid (43 BC to 18 CE). In a French translation of this work, *Ovide moralisé*, done at the beginning of the 14th century, this story of Europa's abduction is interpreted as the abduction of the soul to God.

In the pages that follow we shall look at how Christianity dealt with pre-Christian European culture in the past and see what this can contribute to the effort to convey the Christian message in contemporary European culture. Who will carry off the soul of Europe and where will it be taken?

In 1994 I published a book entitled *Kerstening en ontkerstening van Europa: Wisselwerking tussen Evangelie en cultuur* (literally, "The Christianization and De-Christianization of Europe: The Interplay between Gospel and Culture"). About that time, a well-known Dutch scholar gave a lecture in which he also used the word "Christianization". Surprised when a student in the audience asked what he meant by the term, the lecturer enquired if there were others in the audience who did not understand it. More than half raised their hands.

If such a response is representative for the majority of the Dutch population, then for many the title of my book did not offer much of a clue to what it is about. When it was published in English it was given a title that was more understandable — and provocative: *Europe: Was It Ever Really Christian?* But this in fact touches on only one aspect of my concern. The question that really intrigues me is how far Christianity in the past was able to spread successfully by appropriating much of the pre-Christian culture and religion and whether insight into the history of this can help in presenting the gospel in the secularized Europe of today.

There are two reasons for approaching the topic this way. The first grows out of an observation by the well-known phenomenologist of religion Mircea Eliade that the Christianization of Europe did in fact proceed largely because of the early European church's appropriation of the myths and stories of Europe. But is the reverse also true? If Eliade is correct, I wondered, has the Christian church, by trying to make its message "relevant" through "demythologizing" the gospel, as suggested by the mid-20th-century German New Testament theologian Rudolf Bultmann, in fact blocked rather than promoted a successful communication of the gospel to our contemporaries?

The second reason arises from the question some Third World Christians have posed to European Christians who criticize African and Asian theologians for "syncretism" when they adapt Christianity to African or Asian cultures. The often unanswered counter-question raised by people like the Indonesian Marianne Katoppo or the Ghanaian Kwame Bediako is: exactly how is your theology related to your own European culture?

Edward Schillebeeckx has rightly observed that "there is a constant dialectic between the universality of the gospel, through which it challenges every culture critically and transcends it, and its nevertheless constant appearance in particular cultures".[1] In this connection we may note that the German word *Aufhebung*, which is sometimes used in discussing the relation of the gospel to culture, has a double meaning. It can have the connotation of "abolition", emphasizing the gospel's being at odds with a particular culture, or the connotation of "raising to a new and higher plane". Thus it can point to either affirmation or rejection of the existing culture. Boniface (c. 680-754), "the apostle to the Germans", who was killed at Dokkum in the Netherlands, is a good example of rejection. He literally "put the axe to the roots" of Germanic religion by chopping down the holy Donar oak. A similar example is the missionary Gallus (d. 650), who threw a burning block of wood into a shrine dedicated to Woden on the shores of Lake

Zurich. A case of the other method from about the same time is the instruction of Pope Gregory the Great (c. 540-604) to the missionary to England Augustine of Canterbury that he should not destroy pre-Christian temples but use them to stimulate Christian purposes.

In this short booklet I shall begin by asking how far Europe actually was Christianized during the Middle Ages and how far one can speak of the "de-Christianization" and secularization of Europe in our time. Then, using examples from both Old European and Indo-European (Graeco-Roman, Celtic and Germanic) cultures, I will look at how the Christian church appropriated the pre-Christian culture, especially with reference to sacred places, sacred times and sacred persons. Finally I will address the question of how far the gospel can be communicated in contemporary European culture, taking a cue from past examples. What connection with the "myths" and stories of today can be found? First I will examine one of the realities of modern culture — evolution from a book culture to a visual culture — and the new language this requires. Given this shift, what point of contact for the gospel can be found in our visual culture and visual stories? In addressing this question I will take up both the Reformation critique of the use of images and the contemporary critique of modern visual culture (in particular the "electronic superhighway"). I will ask whether the message can nevertheless be made visual. Then I will turn to the question of whether a way can be found from an attitude of hostility towards myths to a recognition of the truth of myths. I will suggest how the "old, old Story" can be translated authentically into both image and word. Finally, I will argue that word and image should not be placed over against each other, but that both can serve as vehicles for conveying the mystery of the Christian faith in contemporary Europe.

NOTE

[1] E. Schillebeeckx, *Church: The Human Story of God*, tr. J. Bowden, London, 1990, p.36.

1. Christianization, Secularization and European Culture

The coming of Christianity to Europe

It is often assumed that Christianity has existed in Europe for twenty centuries. While it is true that in the 1st century Christianity reached Rome, with the apostles Peter and Paul, and perhaps even Spain if Paul fulfilled his intention to go there, its arrival in other parts of Europe came much later. [1] In the northern part of Europe Christianity spread only slowly, and while Christians travelled to Italy, southern France, Spain and southern England already in the first century, this expansion stagnated with the fall of the Roman empire in the 5th century.

Between 380 and 430 Christianity arrived in Ireland, which had remained outside the Roman sphere of influence and was the only surviving centre of the Celtic world and the Druidic religion, and it was thus present there before the arrival of Patrick, "the apostle of Ireland", in the 5th century. The Irish monks sent missionaries to northern England and were involved in the conversion of Scotland before 600. At the beginning of the 7th century they established themselves on the island of Lindisfarne, off the east coast of Northumbria, from where they further Christianized England. In the 7th century Christianity began to spread in England — about the same time as Islam entered Europe via Spain. The spread of Christianity in central and northern Europe followed the so-called Celtic route, via Ireland and southern England, where Celtic culture had entrenched itself against Roman aggression.

In the seventh and eighth centuries the European continent was Christianized from England. People left their homelands for the sake of Christ (the so-called *peregrinatio propter Christum*). In 1989 the Netherlands commemorated the 1250th anniversary of the arrival of the English missionary Willibrord (c. 658–739). The Scandinavian countries, including Iceland and Finland, were Christianized around the year 1000. East Prussia and the Baltic countries were the last to be converted, around 1200. Christianity became the official religion in Lithuania in 1387.

The most important reason for the expansion of Latin Christianity was military superiority.[2] One thinks first of all in this connection of the conversion to Christianity of Emperor Constantine (d. 337). Political motivations also played a role in the conversion of rulers like the Frankish prince Clovis (466–511). And it is well known that Charlemagne (768–814) did not achieve the conversion of the Saxons without the use of force.

Whereas in the East liturgies in Syrian, Aramean, Armenian and Coptic developed alongside the Greek liturgy, the Latin liturgy prevailed in the West — where Greek was no longer understood after 400. The consequence was that one specific culture and language dominated, and there was no room for a Celtic, Iberian or Punic liturgy.

For the rest, the intensity and degree of the Christianization process in the Middle Ages can be questioned. It has been remarked that the Christianization of Europe was actually completed only at the time of the Reformation and the Counter-Reformation — in other words, at the end of the 16th century. Europe in the Middle Ages was less Christian than is often thought; and at present, perhaps, God is not as dead as is sometimes suggested.

"De-Christianization" and "secularization"

This last remark raises the question of what the current situation is with regard to "*de*-Christianization". Certainly we live in a time when the European world is becoming increasingly secularized. Recent evidence of this came in newspaper reports of research conducted among 7000 people in six countries showing that the most familiar international symbol is the five interlocking rings of the Olympic movement (recognized by 92 percent of those interviewed), followed by the trademarks of Shell Oil and McDonald's (88 percent). Only 54 percent of those interviewed recognized the Christian cross.[3]

The Dutch Socialist prime minister Wim Kok told an interviewer in August 1995 that he had had the cross removed from his office because he was not associated in any way with Roman Catholicism. At the same time Catholics in Bavaria in southern Germany began campaigns to protest the decision by the Constitutional Court in Karlsruhe that crucifixes must be removed from the public schools, since their display conflicted with the freedom of religion inscribed in the German constitution. The court argued that a crucifix has an "appealing" character, pointing to the Christian faith as "exemplary" and worthy of adherence, and that for unbelievers and adherents of non-Christian religions the cross is "the symbol of missionary expansion".[4]

A report by the Dutch Social and Cultural Planning Office on the growing number of non-churchgoers in the Netherlands received considerable media attention in 1994. The projection was made that in the not-too-distant future only 25 percent of the population would belong to a church. These data were reported in such a way as to suggest the survey dealt not only with the decline of church membership but also a decline in belief. Even so, the seriousness of the situation is not to be trivialized. As sociologists are quick to point out, it is not easy for beliefs to remain alive without certain organizational forms, so that a decline in church membership may well have serious consequences for the decline of faith. But the two are not the same.

In any case, no one would deny that something is amiss. It is indeed a problem if our contemporaries no longer understand certain Christian symbols (even if they themselves do not see a problem here), if "holy days" are secularized into mere "holidays" (even granting that the "holy days" of an earlier age also brought with them a sense of vacation). Before the time of Patrick in Ireland, the Druids revered clover as a sacred plant. St Patrick used the clover leaf as an illustration and even a "proof" of the Trinity. He killed snakes with a cruciform staff whose top was shaped like a clover leaf. On Croagh, a mountain in western Ireland, there is a statue of Patrick blessing climbers with the sign of the cross in the form of a clover leaf. But what significance does all this have if these "signs" are no longer understood?

Recently in the Netherlands there has been a discussion concerning questions of meaning, norms and values in contemporary society.[5] People speak of a decline of morality and of a loss of meaning. To what extent do contemporary Europeans still feel that they are living in an "inspirited" context? There is a great deal of talk about the "hiddenness" of God. Speaking of God no longer seems to be taken for granted in many northern European countries.

This process of secularization has in fact been going on in Europe for a long time. Already on the eve of the 20th century Friedrich Nietzsche (d. 1900) wrote of "the death of God". Half a century later, Carl Gustav Jung wrote: "I know — and here I am only expressing what countless other people know — that the present period is the time of God's disappearance and death." Jung concluded that the Christian concept of God had slowly faded from the dreams of his patients, that is, from the unconscious of the modern person. The loss of this image entails the loss of the highest and most powerful factor that gives life meaning.[6]

The question that forces itself upon us at the end of the 20th century is whether we have not entered into an even more advanced phase of this. Is it not the case for many younger people — and for a growing number of older people — at least in northwestern Europe, that the question of meaning is being asked less and less and that there is almost no talk of the quest for God?

What is the reason for this? One study of young people who had left the church in the Netherlands concluded that, at least as far as those interviewed were concerned, their parents seemed to have handed down "an empty testament", an inheritance in which nothing was in fact passed on.[7] Despite outward appearances, the "Reformed-ness" of the Reformed today has no content. The non-religiousness of Reformed young people, their indifference and scepticism towards church and faith, is a continuation of the Reformed heritage of their parents which had no content. According to this research, young people who have left the church are not asking religious questions, questions of meaning and existence; they are concerned with them very little if at all. These young people are non-religious whether one defines religion substantially or functionally. Their non-religiousness, concluded the researcher, "is not independent, but the continuation of a relatively irrelevant religion at home during their primary socialization and upbringing". It is not secularization from outside — the enticements of the world — but rather secularization from within — empty faith — that has led to this falling away.

If the results of this research can be generalized, we can say that for many young people in Dutch society the rites of the Christian faith have become empty and the Christian story, the "myth" which is borne by the rites, no longer has any content.

European cultures

In considering the question of the interplay between the gospel and European culture, one must take account of the double character of pre-Christian Europe: "Indo-European" culture on the one hand and "Old European" culture on the other.

The first date taught to Dutch elementary school children in their history lessons is that "a hundred years before Christ the Batavians entered our country". It is not only into the Low Countries but into all of Europe that various peoples penetrated over the course of the centuries. Through these migrations they established themselves in Europe and spread out over the whole continent. It was in these so-called migrations of peoples that the Indo-Europeans invaded Europe, and a distinction can thus be made between the Old European and Indo-European cultures.

Old European culture flourished for two thousand years from about 6500 to 4500 BC. This was "disrupted" by the arrival of nomads from the East, referred to as Indo-Europeans (or Aryans), who came from the steppes between the Dnieper and Volga rivers. It is only from archaeology that we have a little knowledge of Old European culture before the migrations. Archaeology suggests that the tribal area of the original Indo-European civilization is to be found in the steppes of Pontus between the Black Sea and the Caspian Sea. Indo-European colonization began from Anatolia in the third millennium before Christ. These Indo-Germans or Aryans also penetrated into the Indian subcontinent. They worshipped gods who used thunder and axes and rode on horses.

Only in Greece and on Crete and other Aegean islands were Old European ways of life maintained until as late as 1500 BC. Old European culture was characterized by the worship of nature, the cult of fertility and the central position of the goddess. Their original religion is said to have been a matriarchal, earthly, peaceful and non-hierarchical agricultural religion.

The prominent student of Indo-European culture Georges Dumézil has pointed to the relationship between India and Indo-European culture. As in classical India, three estates of society can be distinguished in Indo-European culture: the concern of the religious estate was for the monarchy and the priests, the concern of the nobility was for the military, while the common people occupied themselves with fertility and well-being.

When one speaks about such diverse European cultures as the Graeco-Roman, Celtic, Germanic or Slavic, for example, one is actually speaking about Indo-European cultures. Whereas the chalice or grail was the symbol of the Old European feminine civilization, according to Riane Eisler, the symbol of Indo-European masculine aggression is the sword. [8]

NOTES

[1] This summary of the spread of Christianity in Europe draws on G.J.M. Bartelink, *De geboorte van Europa: Van laat-Romeins Imperium naar vroege middeleeuwen*, Muiderberg, 1989; and Gerard de Haas, *Publieke religie: Voorchristelijke patronen in ons religieus gedrag*, Baarn, 1994.

[2] Cf. Robert Bartlett, *The Making of Europe*, cited by de Haas, *ibid.*, p.141.

[3] *Ecumenical News International*, No. 16, 15 Aug. 1995, release 95-0312.

[4] *Ibid.*, No. 17, 28 Aug. 1995, release 95-0317.

[5] An account of this discussion is found in P. Fortuyn, *De verweesde samenleving: Achtergronden van en oplossingen voor de huidige normen- en waarden-problemen*, Utrecht, 1995.

[6] Cited in Aniela Jaffé, "Symbolism in the Visual Arts", in Carl Jung and M.L. von Franz (eds.), *Man and his Symbols*, London, 1964, p.255.

[7] Piet van der Ploeg, *Het lege testament: Een onderzoek onder jonge kerkverlaters*, Franeker, 1985, pp.195,199,201.

[8] Riane Eisler, *The Chalice and the Blade: Our History, Our Future*, San Francisco, 1987. On Old European culture and religion, see also M. Gimbutas, "Pre-Historic Religions: Old Europe", in M. Eliade, ed., *The Encyclopaedia of Religion*, New York, 1987; Helmut Uhlig, *Die Mutter Europas: Ursprünge abendländischer Kultur in Alt-Anatolien*, Bergisch Gladbach, 1991; and *Am Anfang war Gott eine Göttin: Eine Weltreligion des Weiblichen*, Bergisch Gladbach, 1992; A. Baring and J. Cashford, *The Myth of the Goddess: Evolution of an Image*, London, 1993.

2. *Appropriating the Sacred*

In order to see how the Christian churches in Europe appropriated the Old European and Indo-European cultures, we will consider the *Aufhebung* of pre-Christian culture and religion as expressed in sacred places, sacred times and sacred persons.

Sacred places

Many examples can be mentioned in which the spirit of Pope Gregory's instruction to Augustine cited earlier — not to destroy the "temples of idols" but to sprinkle them with holy water — was followed. All over Europe Christian churches have been built on pre-Christian sacred places.

The Santa Maria Maggiore in Rome was constructed on the spot where a temple of Juno used to stand. Juno, the goddess who protected women, marriage and birth in ancient Italy, was later identified with the Greek goddess Hera and as the wife of Jupiter. The month of June was dedicated to her.

A good example of how the church appropriated existing worship comes from excavations of a famous shrine to Hera in the ruins of Paestum in southwestern Italy, where archaeologists found many votive offerings, including small images of the enthroned goddess with a child on the left arm and a pomegranate in the right hand. The pomegranate in the hand of Juno was a symbol of marriage in Roman culture. It is, of course, no accident that in the 12th century a church was dedicated to the "Madonna with the pomegranate" near this shrine. The representations of this Madonna and of Hera are completely identical.[1] The pomegranate became a popular sign of Mary.

Notre Dame in Paris was built on the site of a 6th-century church which in turn was built on a shrine dedicated to Osiris. The cathedral of Chartres was built on top of a famous Celtic shrine. At the time Chartres was the city of the Celtic tribes of the Carnutes. The worship of the black Madonna there is said to go back to a Celtic fertility cult which revered "a virgin who will bear". Just as the apostle Paul made a connection with the Athenians' "unknown god"

(Acts 17:23) in his sermon on the Areopagus, the church saw the Celts as "unwittingly" revering Mary in this "virgin who would bear". The Mary pilgrimage to Le Puy in Auvergne, France, has its origin in the earliest times of Christianity. A church was built on the site of a Celtic "stone of fevers", where anyone who lay down to rest (compare the story of Jacob at Bethel in Gen. 28:11) would rise up healthy. The Druidic service was replaced by a Christian one, and this stone is still displayed behind the gilded gate of the Cathedral of Notre Dame in Le Puy. Also sacred to the Druids was the island of Iona, where the Irish pilgrim Columba (521–597) built a monastery which became one of the most important missionary centres of the Celtic church.[2]

The most extreme western point of the European mainland, known as *Finis Terrae*, "the end of the earth", was visited by pilgrims before the apostle James was venerated in Santiago.[3] In the 4th century the church father Jerome asserted confidently that Spain had been Christianized by James, a view shared by Isidore of Seville. James is said to have been buried in Iria, now Galicia, in a cave that had previously been dedicated to Bacchus. Subsequently Santiago de Compostela became one of the best-known centres for Christian pilgrimage.

In German-speaking parts of Europe certain churches built on pre-Christian sacred places are known as *Heidenkirchen* ("pagan churches"). In Alsace there is a church of St Maternus (bishop of Cologne) known as the *Heidenkanzel* ("pagan pulpit"). In Saarland a *Heidenkirche* is situated on the Halberg, and in Tyrol there is a hill known as *Heidenbühel* ("pagan hill"), on which is located a cemetery called *Heidenfriedhof* ("pagan cemetery"). There were churches called *Heidentempel* ("pagan temples") elsewhere as well.[4]

In the extreme west of Ireland, by Clew Bay on the Atlantic Ocean, stands a remarkable mountain that has been holy for thousands of years. Before the coming of Christianity, festivals on its slopes honoured the god Lugh, worshipped by the Celts, whose name survives in the names of Lyons and Laon in France and Leiden in the Netherlands, as well as in the Irish word for August, *Lughnasa*, which is the beginning of the harvest and is celebrated with community feasts.

The Christian transformation of the pre-Christian custom of going to this sacred place is associated with St Patrick. Every year on the last Sunday of July, the so-called "Reek of Garland Sunday", thousands of pilgrims journey to the highest point in the west of Ireland, Croagh Patrick (765 meters). The "Book of Armagh", an early 9th-century manuscript of the New Testament and other writings, relates that Patrick fasted on this mountain in 441. Like Moses on Mount Sinai, Patrick remained here forty days and forty nights. On this hill is also found the so-called bed of Patrick, marked by a pile of stones, where he drove off a witch who tried to enchant him with garlic juice by throwing a bell (which all Celtic missionaries wore) at her head. Pilgrims walk around this spot seven times, praying the Lord's Prayer and the Ave Maria and reciting the creed or confession of faith. The custom of circling a sacred place probably dates from the time when the Irish worshipped the sun.

In the Netherlands, restoration work on the Reformed Church in Elst, near Arnhem, uncovered a Roman shrine. But what is particularly interesting in the Low Countries, perhaps because of their geography, is the association of sacred places with sources of water in an area which is itself so rich in water. The worship of wells could have a Celtic origin.

Holy water played a strikingly significant role in the miracles performed by Willibrord. When his companions were thirsty, Willibrord conjured up fresh water in salt water areas along the coast. In a monastery in Trier where several nuns had died of the plague, Willibrord ended the plague by reading a mass to the sick, sprinkling their home with holy water and allowing those who were sick to drink it. He also used holy water to drive away an evil spirit which had been terrorizing a family. He had all the household goods brought outside and sprinkled with holy water, because he foresaw that the house would go up in flames. The new house, built on the spot which had been sprinkled by holy water, was a safe place to live from that time on.

In the Christian tradition water has been since creation the element of the Holy Spirit, of the rescue of Noah, an image of the church of Christ, of the baptism of Jesus in the Jordan and the baptism of all believers after him. Water was also sacred to the Germans, who celebrated the presence of the divine at wells and brought offerings there. Willibrord's miracles with water, well-suited to the watery regions of Friesland, bore witness to the transfer to a new symbolism, but one in which water is just as holy.

Similar examples of pre-Christian sacred places in northern Europe which are now "occupied" by churches can be found in Jelling, Denmark, and Gamla Uppsala, Sweden, where a wooden temple stood until 1100.[5] Sacred places were also marked by maypoles and labyrinths, which were used in the rites of spring. Before the second world war the villagers in Ootmarsum in the province of Overijsel, in the Netherlands, took part in a serpent-labyrinth dance. In Libussa in Prague there is a labyrinth dance-place.[6]

Sacred times

In European languages such as French, German, English and Dutch, the names of the days of the week betray their pre-Christian religious roots in the Germanic or Roman pantheon.

In English, German and Dutch the names of the first two days of the week are associated with the sun and the moon. Tuesday comes from the Germanic god Tiuz or Tîwaz: the god of court sessions, of friendship contracted with people, the god who fulfils his promises and has made a covenant with the world. Wednesday refers to Woden or Odin, the god who embodies the magical, religious aspect of the highest authority. Thursday is named after Thunor or Thor, the god of war. Friday takes its name from Freya or Frigga, the goddess invoked in matters of love and at the same time the Old European goddess of the fertility of the earth. Saturday is named after Saturn, the Roman god of sowing and reaping. There is also an echo here of "satyrs", the "goat-men" of the lively and exuberant Old European fertility rituals. In French the names of four of the days of the work-week are derived from the Roman pantheon: *mardi* (Mars), *mercredi* (Mercury), *jeudi* (Jupiter), *vendredi* (Venus).

In certain European languages Christianization is explicitly evident in the new names given to some days of the week. Germans call Saturday *Sonnabend*, the eve of Sunday, or *Samstag*, which is derived from the Hebrew *Shabbat*. The French *samedi* has its roots in the Vulgate Latin: *sabbati dies* (day of the sabbath). In Russian Sunday is called "the day of the resurrection".

Christianity's appropriation of existing "sacred times" is particularly striking in the case of festivals. If one were to ask what is the most important Christian feast, the proper theological answer is no doubt Easter, the celebration of Christ's death and resurrection, which is central to the Christian faith. Yet many people, responding at the level of their own experience, would probably be inclined to say that Christmas is the most important. The reason for this, I think, lies in the clear connection the church in Europe sought to make between Christian festivals and already existing Roman and Celtic "sacred times". Since the 4th century, Christmas has been celebrated on 25 December, the festival of the "birth of the invincible sun" (Mithras). In northern Europe it was also primarily the time to celebrate midwinter, which contributed in no small measure to the popularity of the Christian festival. In Scandinavia, it is still called by the pre-Christian name Yule, the main Germanic winter festival.

The other solstice celebration, 21 June, the beginning of the summer, was associated by the church with the feast of Christ's forerunner John the Baptist (24 June). John's words referring to Jesus — "He must increase, but I must decrease" (John 3:30) — were interpreted in terms of the symbolism of the sun, since Christ was seen as the "the sun of righteousness" (Mal. 4:2).

Whereas the Dutch and French words for the festival of the resurrection (*Paasfeest* and *Pâques*, cf. English "paschal") take over the Greek/Hebrew name, in English and German (Easter and *Ostern*) the name is derived from that of Ostara, the goddess of spring. In this connection, we may note that the liturgical or church year follows both a solar and a lunar calendar. The celebration of the birth of Christ, the incarnation, is connected with the solar year and its date is fixed — 25 December. However, the festivals associated with the rites of reconciliation — the death, resurrection and ascension of Christ — are governed by the lunar calendar: the symbol of death and resurrection is the moon, which, in its waxing and waning, is always being reborn. Its rising and setting and continually new shape make it a fitting symbol for death and rebirth. [7]

Another example of such appropriation of pre-Christian sacred times is Candlemas (2 February). In the Celtic world the veneration of St Brigit is celebrated in the same period in which the feast of the goddess Brigit was celebrated. Her feast day is 1 February, *Imbolc*, the beginning of spring in the Irish calendar. On the basis of a decision made by Pope Gelasius I (492–96) it was celebrated as the Candlemas feast. The distribution of cakes has remained an important part of the rites of 1 February. Sometimes the feast is called "The Feast Day of the Bride of the Candles". [8]

All Saints' Day and All Souls' Day were chosen in connection with the important Celtic date *Samhaim*, the beginning of winter and the start of the new year in the Irish calendar. It was believed that during the previous night people had access to the world of the spirits. In 835 the Frankish prince Louis the Pious, on the order of Pope Gregory IV, designated 1 November as All Saints' Day. In 932, the abbot of Cluny established 2 November as All Souls' Day so that ordinary people would not be forgotten.

The festival of Mary's assumption into heaven is 15 August, the day on which the great feast of "Mother Earth" was celebrated in the Old European culture.[9] The earth is seen as the mother of us all. In the creation story in Genesis 2 God took dust from the earth to make the human being, so when we die we return to our mother the earth. This return is celebrated in a real and symbolic way in funeral rites, when the body is laid in the ground and thus again committed to the womb of the earth, the great mother. It has been said that the Old European goddess has continued to exist in the Holy Spirit: "In the third person of the Trinity the goddess of Old Europe has taken up a permanent residence."[10]

All these examples of giving new meaning to certain days and festivals are cases of *Aufhebung*. These dates were fitted into the framework of the liturgical calendar, through which "the community effectively relives the myth of its scripture each year".[11] The old feasts that were celebrated were now associated with the saints. Whereas in the Jewish calendar the celebration of the Sabbath is central to the week and the rest on that day contradicts the idea of connecting not working with an "unlucky day", the Christian church gave a new meaning to the structure of the week through its celebration of the first day of the week, the day of the resurrection, Sunday, the feast of the one who is "the sun of righteousness".

In this connection, it is the notion of the *eighth* day which brings out the most unique aspect of the Christian faith regarding "sacred times". As the "eighth day of creation", the resurrection of Jesus Christ is seen as the beginning of the new age. This is why baptismal fonts are often octagonal, symbolizing the death and resurrection of the person being baptized. The eight-leaved rose windows in Roman art and the eight points of the Maltese cross point in the same direction.

Sacred persons

Various examples may be cited of how the church, in translating the Christian message, took over the stories of "sacred" figures which had previously had a different meaning within their own context. Many pre-Christian divinities became Christian saints: Freya, the goddess of marriage and fertility, became Mary; Balder, the Norse god believed to be invincible, became St Michael; Thor (Thunor), the god of thunder, became St (King) Olaf of Norway; Tonn became St Antony. Destructive divinities in turn were associated with the devil.[12]

The way in which Socrates and Seneca endured their respective deaths was compared with how Christ suffered his. In the Middle Ages, a parallel was drawn between Christ and the Titan Prometheus, who stole fire from heaven. The mystery cult around the mythical singer Orpheus, whose name is related to the word "fish", is said to have played an important role in the shaping of Christianity. One of the figures on an Orphic sacramental bowl from the 3rd or 4th century BCE depicts Orpheus as a "fisher of men" (cf. Luke 5:10) with a fish and a rod at his feet. The Welsh god Bran the Blessed was also called the "fisher of men". His counterpart was the Grail king whom Percival met when he was fishing while waiting for his liberator.

In the ancient Near East and the Mediterranean region Orpheus was associated with the fish, with the great goddess, the archetype of the female, love and fertility. Astarte was also worshipped in the form of a fish. Aphrodite, Venus and Frigga were associated with fish, which was eaten on Friday in order to share in Venus' fertility.

In Judaism fish is viewed as the food of the blessed in Paradise and is eaten during the Sabbath meal. The ancient Jewish symbol of the national restoration that will occur with the coming of the Messiah is a great fish on which the righteous will feast. Three fish with one head or three fish attached to one another, found in the iconography of Mesopotamia, Egypt, India and Persia, is a universal symbol of unity in threeness and represents Christian baptism. The one baptized is immersed in the font, the *piscina*, literally, fish pool. Fish represent resurrection and regeneration.[13]

The church took Theseus, who killed the Minotaur (the half-human, half-bull monster) in the labyrinth, as a prototype of Christ who conquers Satan, is resurrected and brings eternal life to all. Theseus' dance around the horned altar is the prototype of early Christian dances. The labyrinths of Chartres (the floor labyrinth has a diameter of twelve metres) and Auxerre point to the continued existence of this ancient symbolism. [14]

In Christian proclamation the story of the sacrifice of Alcestes (the subject of a drama by the 5th-century BCE Greek tragedian Euripides) was used frequently. Alcestes gave her life for her husband — an idea that is also present in the gospel: "No one has greater love than this, to lay down one's life for one's friends" (John 15:13).

A prominent place in the *Aufhebung* of the worship of goddesses, of course, was occupied by Mary. The cult of the ancient Egyptian goddess Isis, the divine mother of Horus and the protectress of the dead, had a considerable influence on the cult of the virgin Mary. Not until the 6th century CE was the temple of Isis on the island of Philae in Egypt closed by order of the emperor Justinian (527–65). Most of the sacred places for goddesses around the Mediterranean were taken over by Mary. Between 400 and 500 the temple of Isis in Soissons in France was dedicated to the virgin Mary. Between 500 and 600 the temple of Athena, the Parthenon, became a church of Mary. [15]

As the mother of Jesus, the son of God, Mary can easily be seen within the same sphere as the mother goddess cults in the Roman empire, particularly the cult of Isis. Mary as the mother of the resurrected one was finally declared by the Council of Ephesus in 531 to be the queen of heaven and the mother of God (*theotokos*). She takes over the signs and symbols of such other virgin-mother figures as Isis and Astarte. As to the threefold Diana, to Mary also is ascribed the threefold aspect of Virgin, Mother and Queen.

In Ephesus there was a famous temple of Artemis, whom the Romans identified with the Italian moon goddess Diana.

The silversmith Demetrius (Acts 19:21-41) dealt in silver replicas of this temple for the many tourists attracted by it to Ephesus. Artemis here represents the "mother-goddess", the symbol of fertility. Under her name a fertility goddess of Asia Minor was worshipped, depicted as a nursing mother with twenty or more breasts. "Great is Artemis of the Ephesians!" was the usual form of the obligatory invocation to the deity (Acts 19:28,34). With the arrival of Paul and his message that "gods made with hands are not gods at all" (Acts 19:26), Demetrius saw his income and employment put at risk.

Even now one can see the house in Ephesus where Mary is said to have stayed with John. The location of this house in Ephesus suggests that, because of the importance of this earlier worship of the mother-goddess, Mary, as it were, *must have lived* in Ephesus. The cult of Artemis or Diana, which was suppressed in 380 by Emperor Theodosius I, metamorphosed into that of Mary.

Among the most venerated shrines in the Middle Ages were those to the "black virgin" in Chartres (France) and Czestochowa (Poland). Mary is now venerated wherever Isis, Minerva or Athena were worshipped. Their shrines were rededicated to her. This is not to say that all shrines to Mary have pre-Christian roots. From the 12th century on, the veneration of Mary underwent further development in Europe.

St Brigit, next to Patrick the most important saint in Ireland, is said to have lived around the year 600.[16] She is known as the great abbess of the convent of Kildare (*Cill Dara*), which she founded, a leader of the church, the Gaelic Mary and even the second mother of Christ himself. St Brigit has assumed many characteristics of the pre-Christian Celtic goddess Brigit, who with her two sisters was associated with the arts of healing and ironwork.

What remains of the pre-Christian symbolism in the cult of St Brigit is the particular meaning of light and fire. When as an infant she was left in the house on her own, the neighbours saw flames rising from the house and thought it was on fire, but when they looked closer, both the house and the child were unharmed. This motif recalls the Old Testament account of the three men thrown by Nebuchadnezzar into the fiery furnace (Dan. 3) and of Moses and the burning bush (Ex. 3). The fire is kept burning in Brigit's shrine, as was the case also with the Vestal Virgins.

The cross associated with Brigit seems to be linked to one of the symbols of the sun-god. Such crosses, made of rushes and straw and traditionally attached to the rafters of houses, would bring the family luck and blessing in the coming year.

Dorothy Ann Bray says of St Brigit that, "as a native saint with culturally familiar characteristics, she provided the church of Kildare with a means of entrenching Christianity in Irish society and provided a continuity on a popular level for long and widely held beliefs".[17]

The popularity of stories about the Grail in England and Wales as well as continental Europe has to do with the continuation of an old Celtic legend about a vat that produced wonderful food. These stories became popular at a time when the importance of Christian communion as well as the veneration of Mary was increasing.[18]

The connections between pre-Christian and Christian culture are richly illustrated in Christian art. Many images were taken over from Graeco-Roman antiquity into the Christian church. Jonah resting under the bush (Jonah 4:6ff.) was portrayed with an image borrowed from the depiction of Dionysus under the vine or of the sleeping Endymion, loved by the moon goddess, who kissed him to sleep every evening and asked that he might remain eternally young. Prometheus was a model for portraying the creation of humanity and Hercules for Samson's fight with the lion (Judg. 14:5f.). The ascension of Elijah (2 Kings 2:11f.) found its prototype in the sun-god in his chariot.

There are various traces of Christianity assuming a uniquely Celtic hue. The zodiac in the high cross, which symbolizes the sun and the earth, is divided into two and transected by the Christian cross of redemption. The decorations on the high crosses, the interlace of circles and spirals, the so-called Celtic knot, stem from pre-Christian times. Since they have no beginning and no end, they symbolize eternity. Moreover, the Celtic Christians believed that the devil could be warded off by something that had no definite beginning or end.

It is evident from the foregoing that during the period of early Christianization, the church in Europe was able to appropriate already existing stories of sacred places, times and persons. The Christian message took on the colour of its European environment: it was understood and interpreted in this new European context in such a way that what preceded it still sounded through. People sought connections with it. Besides "discontinuity" there was also "continuity". At the same time this *Aufhebung* meant that the church tried to render in this context what was new and unique in its own message.

NOTES

[1] A.R.A. van Aken, *Elseviers Mythologische Encyclopedia*, Amsterdam and Brussels, 1961, p.91. For the appropriation of places sacred to pre-Christian religions in Europe, I have also drawn on Ben Wasser, *Pelgrimages: Bedevaarten van de westerse christenheid*, Nijmegen, 1993; A.G. Weiler, *Willibords missie: Christendom en cultuur in de zevende en achtste eeuw*, Hilversum, 1989; and K. Maurer, "Über die Wasserweihe des germanischen Heidenthums", *Abhandlungen der Philosophisch-Philologischen Classe der königlichen Bayerischen Akademie der Wissenschaften*, Vol. 15, 1881, pp.173-253.

[2] Anthony Duncan, *The Elements of Celtic Christianity*, Shaftesbury, Rockport MA and Brisbane, 1992, p.31.

[3] For the history of the link between St James and Santiago de Compostela, see Michael Jacobs, *The Road to Santiago de Compostela* (Penguin Architectural Guides for Travellers), London, 1991, pp.1-8.

[4] P. Jones and N. Pennick, *A History of Pagan Europe*, London and New York, 1995, p.160.
[5] *Ibid.*, p.121.
[6] *Ibid.*, pp.119, 159, 161.
[7] Cf. Alan Watts, *Myth and Ritual in Christianity*, London, 1954, p.126.
[8] Mary Condren, *The Serpent and the Goddess: Women, Religion and Power in Celtic Ireland*, New York, 1989, pp.73f.
[9] Cf. Duncan, *op. cit.*, p.15, who notes that Carl Jung saw the doctrine of the Virgin Mary's being taken up into heaven as a powerful symbol that could help to restore the lost balance to a society dominated by men and denying women.
[10] De Haas, *Publieke religie*, pp.106f.
[11] W.C. Smith, *What Is Scripture? A Comparative Approach*, London, 1993, p.109.
[12] Jones and Pennick, *op. cit.*, p.160.
[13] Cf. Eliade, *s.v.* "Fish", in *Encyclopaedia of Religion*.
[14] P.R. Doob, *The Idea of the Labyrinth from Classical Antiquity through the Middle Ages*, Ithaca and London, 1990, pp.123ff.; cf. Baring and Cashford, *The Myth of the Goddess*, p.137.
[15] Baring and Cashford, *ibid.*, p.551.
[16] For a more extended treatment of St Brigit, see A. Wessels, *Europe: Was It Ever Really Christian?*, London, 1994, pp.68-73; cf. Dorothy Ann Bray, "St Brigit and the Fire from Heaven", *Études Celtiques*, Vol. 29, 1992, pp.105-112: I owe this reference to Jacqueline Borsje; Condren, *The Serpent and the Goddess*, p.66; Bernard Maier, "Brigit", in *Lexikon der keltischen Religion und Kultur*, Stuttgart, 1994.
[17] *Op. cit.*, p.112.
[18] Jones and Pennick, *op. cit.*, p.162.

3. The Gospel and Contemporary European Culture

Can we draw on the examples of successful appropriation of sacred places, times and persons cited in the previous chapter in seeking a way to convey the gospel within the contemporary European culture?

From book to image

In order to answer that question, we must specify which particular aspect of modern culture we are talking about. Here of course there are many possibilities that can be investigated. One important area which is certainly worth exploring is popular music. One could begin by looking into the ways in which the church in the past sought to appropriate the music of its time — how certain popular melodies of the 16th century found their way into the church and how the organ moved from its secular use in the marketplace to the sacred space of the church.

Or one could draw a parallel between the connection made in the past between the Christian message of Christ and certain figures and the way in which something similar is done in the literature of more recent times. To mention two examples at random, the German writer Thomas Mann (1875–1955) was inspired by the biblical story of Joseph in his famous work *Joseph und seine Brüder*, whereas the Irish author James Joyce (1882–1941), in *Finnegan's Wake*, drew heavily on his knowledge of such figures from Irish history as Kevin of Glendalough and Patrick.

I will not pursue such examples here but will rather focus on another very important aspect of modern culture: the fact that it is a *visual* culture.

In the course of history one can identify important transitions which culture has undergone. I want to point to three of these. The first took place in the 5th century BCE, when Athens changed from being an oral culture to one using an alphabet. It was a tremendous discovery and advance that such a simple system as the alphabet could be used for writing.

The second occurred in the 16th century: the radical transformation Europe underwent as a consequence of the invention of the printing press by Johannes Gutenberg. The resulting spread of the printed world signalled a whole new era — "the Gutenberg era". The transition from image to book had been made.

On 28 December 1895 a cultural upheaval began. On that day in Paris 35 people constituted the first cinema audience in history. The audio-visual culture was born. Gabriel Marcel spoke of the birth of a new type of human being, the *homo spectans*. This third great transition has taken hold in our time as a result of the electronic revolution, in particular the invention of television. The transition was made from a "book" culture to a new "visual" culture.

It is on this third transition that I shall focus here.

Assessment of the image

To see how the gospel might be communicated by seeking links with visual culture, we should begin by looking at how the church dealt with the visual in the past. It is important to establish at the outset that the church has long sought such connections with images and symbols.

If we look to the Middle Ages, we see that the church succeeded uniquely in relating to the visual culture of that time. The mediaeval Christian church used images as "books for the laity". The French writer Victor Hugo (1802–85) observed that whatever was thought to be important in the Middle Ages was inscribed in stone. The cathedral was thus a kind of "book". The encyclopaedic character of mediaeval art is expressed, for example, in the cathedral of Chartres. Amiens is a Messianic, prophetic cathedral. The prophets on the façade, like sentries on the buttresses, look into the future. They speak of the approaching advent of the Redeemer. Notre Dame in Paris is the church of the holy Virgin. In the centrepieces of the two great stained-glass rose windows are, on the one, the saints of the Old Testament and, on the other, the rhythm of different activities, successive months and the forms of the virtues. The cathedral of Laon is one of intellect. The liberal arts, accompanied by philosophy, are sculpted on the façade and portrayed on one of the rose windows. The Scripture is represented in its most profound form: the truths of the New Testament are hidden under the symbols of the Old. Reims is the national cathedral — if the other cathedrals are Catholic, this one is French! The baptism of Clovis is a dominant theme. Bourges celebrates the virtues of the saints: its windows illustrate the Golden Legend. The life and death of the apostles, confessors and martyrs form a sparkling crown around the altar. The portal of Lyons displays the miracles of creation.

Art historian Emile Mâle writes:

> By means of the images and windows of the church, the mediaeval clergy attempted to bring as many truths as possible to believers... For the great illiterate mass, for ordinary people, who possessed neither psalm book nor missal and only remembered those aspects of Christianity which they *saw*, the idea had to be concretized, clothed in a form that could be perceived with the senses. In the 12th and 13th centuries doctrine was also personified in the characters of the liturgical drama and the statues of the church portals, or, to put it again in the words of Victor Hugo: the cathedral was a stone book for the ignorant, which was gradually made superfluous by the printed book. "The Gothic sun set behind the gigantic press of Mainz."[1]

The 16th-century Reformers were well aware of what the times called for, and in the culture that was being born they made good use of the new medium of the book. At the same time, the Reformation opposed the way in which the church of the Middle Ages had used images. Typical is the way the Heidelberg Catechism (Q. & A. 98) interprets the prohibition in the Decalogue of "graven images". The answer of the catechism to the question of whether images may be permitted in the churches as "books for the laity" is: "No, we should not try to be wiser than God. He wants his people instructed by the living preaching of his Word — not by idols that cannot even talk."

It is interesting to note the biblical texts which the catechism cites in the footnotes to support this position. The

Old Testament references deal with God and idols: "They [the wise ones of the nations] are both stupid and foolish; the instruction given by idols is no better than wood!" (Jer. 10:8). "What use is an idol once its maker has shaped it — a cast image, a teacher of lies? For its maker trusts in what has been made, though the product is only an idol that cannot speak!" (Hab. 2:18). The references cited from the New Testament underscore the importance the Reformation gave to *sola scriptura*: "And how are they to hear without someone to proclaim [Christ]?" (Rom. 10:14). "Faith comes from what is heard" (Rom. 10:17). And finally: "So we have the prophetic message more fully confirmed. You will do well to be attentive to this" (2 Pet. 1:19).

It is very questionable whether the appeal to these texts in fact does justice to what the Catholic Church in mediaeval Europe intended by translating the Christian message into images. Being able to "read" the "books for the laity" in fact required a great deal of knowledge, particularly of scripture.

It seems to me that this classic Reformation emphasis makes it difficult for Protestants even today to take a positive stance towards conveying the gospel in the visual culture in which we now live. Reservations about dealing with images persist in Protestant circles, where one can still hear echoes of what the Dutch theologian and politician Abraham Kuyper (d. 1920) wrote in his commentary on the part of the Heidelberg Catechism cited above:

> Almost all peoples who have wrapped the Christian religion in linen and swaddling clothes have become ethically relaxed and broken. On this point Spain and Portugal, all South America and Mexico, Italy and in part even France can by far not stand up to comparison with Prussia, England and the United States. Even the whole Eastern Church has yielded to Islam on this point. The veneration of images leads inevitably in my opinion to *pagan* use and this sinful indulgence of the sensual inclination of our nature also in sacred matters breaks the power of *spiritual* medicine which is offered to us in the Christian religion.[2]

Today these sentiments are expressed in such terms as "the tyranny of the image". Culturally pessimistic theologians — particularly Protestants, with their *sola scriptura* — regard the triumph of the audio-visual as a "humiliation of the word".[3]

Such an attitude does not give Protestant Christians the disposition to be very creative in dealing with visual culture as it has developed in this century. Sylvain de Bleeckere, who has published widely on the theme of visual culture, puts it more strongly and more generally, arguing that during the last five centuries both the Protestant and Roman Catholic churches have followed a cultural line of hostility towards images.[4]

The electronic superhighway

Similar anxiety about visual culture was vividly expressed in a long television programme produced in the Netherlands by the liberal Protestant broadcasting society VPRO, which dealt with questions concerning our current media culture. A specialist on the "electronic superhighway" pointed out that the fate of our culture is now in the hands of a small number of people, the powerful media owners like Rupert Murdoch and Silvio Berlusconi. He spoke of a culture of "distractions", of diversions, and how our culture is being trivialized and impoverished through that process. What is sought by the mass media is not so much an audience as consumers. "You are what you consume" — the right car, the right deodorant, etc. As a result, warned this specialist, the "cultural ecology" of the planet is in danger. Cultural corruption, it was said, is more dangerous than the atom bomb.

There was even talk of a "cultural holocaust". In the past there were certain institutions in culture — the family, religion, civil authority, education. Today, our culture often lacks any belief or moral authority. *The* institution of today is Business. "Everything is marketing." The message, the ideology, is that you must win, not lose. There is an obsessive desire to score ("ratings"). Everything is centred on commercial communication. The Berlusconis of this world are not interested in serving the public interest: private interests are more important than the public interest. Public interest is merely that in which the public is interested. Discussion of values is almost non-existent.

These criticisms echo what Neil Postman wrote in *Amusing Ourselves to Death*, a book which investigates — and laments — the most important development in US cultural life in the second half of the 20th century: the decline of the Age of Typography and the ascendancy of the Age of Television. "As the influence of print wanes, the content and meaning of politics, religion, education and anything else that comprises public business must change and be recast in terms that are most suitable to television." The sole purpose of television programming in the USA is entertainment. However, the problem with television is not that entertainment is offered but that *every* programme, whatever the topic, must be presented as entertainment.

Amusement, to use Postman's term, is the super-ideology of television discourse. The stories collected and broadcast on television news programmes are not intended to be *read* but to be *seen*. It is forbidden to say on television, "I'll have to think about that", or, "I don't know". Such discourse is detrimental to the show. Thinking does not come across well on television — it is not sufficiently theatrical. The bottom line is that television is *watched* — it is not for nothing that it is called tele*vision*. The nature of the medium is such that the content is completely subordinated to the visual. Consequently, the prevailing norms and values are those which determine everything in show business. So pervasive has this influence become in the USA that in courts, schools, operating rooms, boardrooms, churches and even airplanes people no longer converse with one another, they "entertain" each other. They exchange not thoughts but impressions. They no longer try to convince each other with arguments but by appealing to superficialities like celebrities and advertising slogans.

Postman mentions a number of features of television that stand in the way of religious experience. The first is that the space in which a television programme is watched cannot be consecrated. Our behaviour needs to be in accordance with consecrated space; watching television does not normally meet the conditions for this. In addition, the television screen itself has a strong anti-religious aura. It is so permeated by thoughts of worldly events, so strongly associated with the realm of commerce and entertainment, that it is difficult to transform it into a framework for religious activities. The unwritten law of television preaching is that you will get people to watch your programme only if you give them what they are asking for. Every great religious leader — whether Buddha, Moses, Jesus, Mohammed or Luther — has given people not what they were asking for but what they needed, Postman argues. But television is not suited to giving people what they need; it is "user-friendly". Television cannot tolerate complex language and the issuing of stringent demands. The Sermon on the Mount or something similar could not be preached on television. But if the gospel is proclaimed in an easy and entertaining way, then Christianity is no longer Christianity.

The evil does not lie in *what* we watch but in *that* we watch. The solution must be sought in the attitude to watching. I believe it can be said that we still have to learn what television is. If the fear of George Orwell in *1984* was that books would be banned, the worry of novelist, essayist and poet Aldous Huxley in *Brave New World* was that there would not be any reason to ban books. Orwell was afraid that the truth would be hidden from us, Huxley that it would be drowned in a sea of triviality.[5]

The criticisms expressed in the Dutch television programme cited earlier and in Neil Postman's book must be taken seriously. It is undeniable that the media culture is ambivalent. The images that are employed are not all that innocent. There are myths that need to be combatted, such as the antisemitic myth that flourished in the 1930s in Europe, notably given expression in Alfred Rosenberg's *The Myth of the Twentieth Century* (1930). Rosenberg was the favourite ideologist of National Socialism, and in his work he elaborated on the racial theories of De Gobineau and H. St Chamberlain to try to demonstrate the inequality of the races and give antisemitism a scientific guise.

That images in the media are not innocent can be illustrated by the function of the cartoon character Donald Duck. According to Robert W. Brockway, Donald Duck cartoons may well be seen as a manifestation of capitalism as it is practised in the USA. In a subtle way people all over the world can thus be indoctrinated into the ideology, myths and illusions of the "American dream". Mickey Mouse and Donald Duck are the *avatars* of that dream. Walt Disney's productions smooth over the hard realities of global capitalism, indoctrinating and seducing. Disney's creations are intended to function as palliatives and to create the illusion that those in power are benefactors. Disney's *Snow White and the Seven Dwarfs* differs from the original fairy tale as told by the Brothers Grimm in its sweetness and charm. It teaches the capitalist ethos with songs like "Whistle while you work" and "Heigh-ho, heigh-ho, it's off to work we go!". Because of the great artistry of the original drawings, this film became in the 1930s as effective for capitalism as the Gothic cathedrals and stained-glass windows were for mediaeval Christianity. Disneyland has appropriately been called "a cathedral of capitalism".[6]

Of course, it is true that developments in any culture, of whatever age, can be ambivalent. Consider for example the discovery at the beginning of the Bronze Age (3500 to 1250 BCE) that mixing copper and tin produced an alloy that is more flexible and durable. In the river valleys of these early civilizations bronze was used to cast ploughs that were a significant improvement on primitive wooden ploughs. But there were other applications of this discovery as well.

Bronze swords and battle axes would not break in combat and thus were more effective in seriously wounding and killing an enemy.

There is little sense in only complaining about the developments in a culture. Once a particular discovery or invention is made, the challenge that confronts humankind is the same: how to use it well. It is clear that one can take a positive or negative attitude towards our visual culture. That was the case also in the Bronze Age. One could either take up the sword or beat one's swords into ploughshares, as in the vision of a prophet from this period (Micah 4:3).

There is certainly an urgent need today for a "critical hermeneutic of the media". One of the questions it will pose is who dominates the media and whose interests the media serve. Another evidence of the ambivalence of the media is the way in which their orientation to pure entertainment enables comfortable people in the First World to take the role of mere spectators of famine in Africa, floods in Bangladesh or war in the Balkans. They want to be entertained by something new, but they are not moved or stimulated to act.[7] Such people resemble the figure Rembrandt portrays in his so-called *Hundred Guilder Print*, an etching which depicts what is recorded in Matthew 19. Jesus' blessing the children is the main scene, but also present are the sick waiting to be healed, the Pharisees discussing how they can trap Jesus and the rich young ruler. Jesus stands in the middle as a benefactor who heals, teaches and calls people to follow him. But, as Rembrandt sometimes does, there is one figure depicted who is not mentioned in Matthew 19. He is in the foreground with his hands behind his back, just watching. He does not get involved; he is purely a spectator, an "observer".

But while a critical stance is necessary in the face of the misuse of the media culture, one must also reflect on how it can be used positively, including its potential for communicating the gospel.

In this connection it has been observed that there is a specific audio-visual mode of expression and experience. As media expert Henk Hoekstra points out, over against conceptual language with its words and ideas, audio-visual language works primarily not with a *rational* but an *affective* logic:

> For that reason this audio-visual language does not lend itself so much to rational, intellectual argumentation as to telling stories and portraying dramas. Film and television, as audio-visual media, make use of the drama model of communication. The drama model does not correspond to the rational model; on the contrary, it has to do with a plot and proceeds from a conflict. Fundamentally, all television programmes are dramas or mini-dramas. [8]

People now speak of a "symbolic communicative environment" which is created by the various media and their messages. We are obliged today to live in three worlds at the same time: the natural environment, the social and cultural environment, and the communicative or symbolic environment. This communicative symbolic environment has become so important that we can solve the problems of the other two worlds only with its help. In Hoekstra's words, "our symbolic universe is a universe full of messages, announcements, pronouncements, invitations, appeals and information, which concern life and society". [9]

Television has made an essential contribution to the return of myth. To express this understanding of reality, audio-visual language often avails itself of primal symbols, archetypes, rites and cults. The argumentation is much more general and accessible to people. It is no surprise that television and audio-visual language is so appealing to working people, children and the elderly. In verbal culture it was important *what* was said and *how* it was argued and *what conclusions* were drawn. Rational argumentation was central. In the age of television primary importance is ascribed to *who* says something. Can he or she be trusted? If one's judgment about that person is positive, one can also believe what he or she says. In audio-visual culture the person takes precedence over the issue, whereas in verbal culture it is the other way around.

We no longer live in the Gutenberg era but in a visual culture. The old answer is not adequate for the challenges of today. Are we as church in a position to use the new media and audio-visual language? The form is newer than the content. More important than *what* is said is *who* says it. In the visual culture *credibility* is more important than *belief*.

Although the Reformers appealed to scripture to emphasize "hearing", other accents can also be pointed out. Perhaps it is good in our changed culture to remember what is written in Proverbs: "The hearing ear and the seeing eye — the Lord has made them both" (Prov. 20:12). The Psalmist urges us to "taste and *see* that the Lord is good" (Ps. 34:8). Next to its emphasis on listening, the New Testament also mentions seeing: "Truly I tell you, many prophets and righteous people longed to see what you see, but did not see it" (Matt. 13:17). Attention should be given not only to the hearing of the word (*ex auditu*) — under the influence of the epistle to the Romans (10:17) — but to *seeing* as well. The use of icons shows that the Orthodox churches have understood this well. Seeing the beauty of the Roman liturgy played an important role in attracting the Germans and motivating their conversion.

The church in our time must explore the question of how to turn the "electronic superhighway" into "a way of the Lord".

Hoekstra quite rightly resists playing off one form of communication (that of the visual culture) against the other (that of the verbal culture). He acknowledges that a verbal culture can be very imaginative, whereas a culture of audio-visual images nevertheless implies the word. The two are complementary forms of communication, and both are needed.

A recent essay in *Concilium* offers a useful caution against a one-sided approach in this area. "Radical" Christians are sometimes inclined to argue that all the stories and symbols of contemporary culture are characterized by an ideology of domination, so that if they are used in religious communication, they will have the ideological function of reconciling people to society as it is. I would suggest that such an apodictic judgment needs to be corrected by the view traditionally associated with "liberal" Christians that God is always at work among people, even before the word of the church reaches them. The culture of our time is made up of all kinds of layers and traditions, and some of them are the expression of the redemptive dramas of human existence: the restoration of the downtrodden, the liberation of the imprisoned, the passing over from darkness to light, the joy of an unexpected and undeserved gift, the resurrection of the dead. Here God is present with God's grace. These dramas play themselves out among us: they do not mirror the thinking and action of the world, but liberate us from the world. These dramas have, like the gospel itself, something paradoxical about them: they are both alien and not alien to modern society. Because God is present in the struggles of human existence and our attempts to express them, Christians are able to use the communication media to pass on the gospel in the language of contemporary culture. [10]

In the 13th century, Helène Noltenhuis has suggested, Francis of Assisi saw "a gap in the market" and became the first to preach in intelligible *images* in the simple language of the poor. [11] Similarly, the church in Europe today must try to find ways to link up with the culture of images — now the culture of audio-visual images. Every age has the task of writing its own "fifth gospel". The "law of evangelization" is to pass on the good news in the language of the culture in which people live. [12]

Sunrise over Mainz?

How then can the gospel be communicated at a time when the book culture is giving way to a visual culture? If the cathedral of the Middle Ages was the "book" in which the message was "read", viewed by and communicated to the people, can something similar obtain in our time? Earlier we cited Victor Hugo's remark that with Gutenberg's invention of the printing press the Gothic sun set behind Mainz. In our time a new example of the communication of the Christian gospel can be found in the very same city, created by that versatile 20th-century artist Marc Chagall. Has the "Gothic sun", one might ask, now risen again in Mainz?

This famous artist of Russian Jewish origins has provided many churches in Europe, including that of Reims in France, with artistic representations proclaiming and explaining the Christian message in stained-glass windows using symbols from both the Old and New Testaments.

In 1973 the Rev. Klaus Mayer went to Chagall, as "the master of colour and the biblical message", with a commission to place in the east choir of the St Stephanskirche in Mainz a symbol of German-French friendship, the understanding among the peoples of "the peace that is so necessary for our life". Chagall wanted to place a symbol of Jewish-Christian affinity in a Christian church in Germany.[13] The first window finished was the centre one, with a representation of the God of the ancestors, "the God of Abraham, Isaac and Jacob". Here the viewer is made aware that the God of our Lord Jesus Christ is none other than the "God of the fathers" to whom the New Testament scriptures testify. The window is in blue, a meditative colour, and exudes a wonderful calm. Those who surrender themselves to its predominant colour experience rest and sense a hint of what mystery is.

In the flanking windows Chagall broadened his vision from the "God of the fathers" to the history of salvation, beginning with the image of creation and finishing with an image of the eternal Sabbath, the fulfillment. These windows depict more movement than the centre window, for the history of God with God's creation is full of the flow of life. For the most part, the chosen people are somewhat larger than in the centre window, because they stand in the forefront of the history of salvation. In the centre window the forms are smaller, the blue patches larger. For the further the artist ventures into the mystery of God the smaller and more insignificant becomes what happens in the foreground.

Two *leitmotifs* stand out. One is the covenant God has made with the whole of creation. God states: "I have set my bow in the clouds, and it shall be a sign of the covenant between me and the earth" (Gen. 9:13) — a universal and eternal covenant. The other (probably used for the first time as a motif in stained-glass windows) is that of woman. Chagall reproduces not only the role of *man* in salvation history but gives the same space and importance to the role of *woman*. While the north window is called the window of the woman and the southeast window the window of the man, men can be seen in the window of the woman and women in the window of the man. The point is that creation and salvation history are not a matter of the sexes alongside each other but of their being *with* each other, their polarity. The two windows portray the dialogue of the biblical couple, redeemer and redemptrix, prophetess and prophet, king and queen, Christ and Mary.

What is evident here is how much Christ in his humanity is rooted in the Jewish people and its history. Chagall shows Mary nursing the child and indicates her election (Luke 1:26-38 — the annunciation). The crucified one is the Christ exalted on the cross. From there Chagall jumps back to Sarah, the matriarch of Israel (Gen. 16:1; 17:1-22), and shows a praying child, thus drawing a link to the centre window, for the visit of the three angels to Abraham quickly follows. At the same time there is an internal connection to the Christ image: "By your offspring shall all the nations of the earth gain blessing for themselves" (Gen. 22:18). There is the completion. Above Christ are the tablets of the covenant, in red and placed in such a way as to show that all of God's creation and all of God's instruction well up out of God's love (Deut. 6:47). Elsewhere one can see the lights — a symbol for the sabbath. The seventh day (Gen. 2:23) is represented as diagonal to the portrayal of creation to evoke the passing someday into the eternal sabbath, the fulfillment, when the covenant with God, the creation and with it we the people, man and woman, will find completion.

But word and image, as we said, are not to be played off against each other. Just as the Ethiopian needed Philip to explain to him what he was reading (Acts 8:31), so the people in the cathedrals of the Middle Ages and visitors to the Stephanskirche in Mainz today need someone to explain the art to them. The latter can be experienced as a contemporary pilgrimage in which, by way of the light-blue-coloured windows on the side, one is introduced and initiated further into the mystery as it is represented in the deep blue windows above the main altar.

Seeking the truth of contemporary myth

What can we learn from the past about paving a way "from demythologization to the truth of the myth"?[14] To clarify what is meant here, we must first take up the question of what is understood by "myth".

The growing hostility to myth in the 20th century is well known. The word is usually used to mean a story that is not true. And the myths of antiquity have been trivially dismissed as "highly poetical talk about the weather".[15] In this connection we may note in passing an interesting shift in the Netherlands in the course of a single generation. The disastrous floods of 1953 elicited a good deal of discussion about divine providence. By contrast, the serious flooding which threatened to break through the dikes in January and February 1995 was explained in a purely secular way: it was the government in The Hague (or Bonn) that was held responsible. To be sure, these two kinds of explanation need not represent mutually exclusive alternatives, but in fact the appeal to God's providence in connection with a disaster or threat of a disaster does not arise in the secular approach. Perhaps, indeed, the myths of a time do speak about more than just the weather.

In discussing the meaning of myth it is worth remembering that the Greek philosopher Aristotle was called a *philomythos*, a lover of stories. In his *Poetics* (51a36) he says that the (made-up) stories of the poets, the epics and the tragedies, contain more truth than do faithful descriptions of factual reality by the historians. Historiography is a report of particular and accidental facts, whereas poetry speaks about general structures of existence and about the possible and the necessary. The poetic word, Aristotle goes on, is thus also closer to philosophy than the description of facts is.

As an historian of philosophy, Aristotle observed that the new "natural" way of thinking — over against the old mythical or theological way — began with Thales of Miletus (d. ca. 545 BCE) and the other Milesian thinkers. Aristotle himself had an eye not only for the distinction but also for the entwining and combining of the mythical and the rational, as shown by his formula "reproducing theories in a mythical way". Unfortunately, according to the philosopher and anthropologist Johannes Blauw (to whom I owe these references), this insight is largely missing today, primarily because of the pressure of 18th-century rationalism. It has given way to a belief in a radical division between the mythical and the rational. For rationalism, "mythical thinking" represents images, figures and concrete forms that exclude intellectual concepts, while "rational thinking" represents thinking about the concepts in a logical context. In addition, under the influence of F.W.J. von Schelling (1775-1854) and G.W.F. Hegel (1770-1831) the idea arose of "an evolution from more primitive, mythical forms of thought to more developed, rational forms of thought".[16]

In our century Carl Jung and Sigmund Freud completely revolutionized perspectives on myths and showed how they were related to dreams and fantasies. They also demonstrated that, far from disappearing with the Enlightenment, myth has continued to persist in our civilization, disguised in literature, art and popular culture. Jungian psychologists hold that both myths and fairy tales reveal archetypes of the collective unconscious. The folk tale or fairy tale can be described as a myth of a lower kind, and the fairy tale can be an introduction to the imaginative language of the soul. Friedrich von Schiller (1759-1805) once said: "The fairy tales told to me in my youth contain a deeper content than the truth that life teaches."[17]

Where myths are still living symbols, similar mythological images are encountered in our dreams. "But where theologians have appeared with a notepad in their hands, and have managed to have their say, the metaphors have been fossilized into statements. Mythology is then read wrongly as a direct report or science; the symbol becomes a fact, metaphor a dogma."[18]

The British Christian writers G.K. Chesterton (1874-1936) and C.S. Lewis (1898-1963) described fairy tales as "spiritual explorations". A careful distinction was made between fairy tales and myths and their use. Fairy tales are intended for adults and for the somewhat older child. Fairy tales form the mythology of the middle phase of childhood and answer the psychological needs of this period, just as myths respond to the needs of the culture in which they continue to live. The nursery rhymes of Mother Goose, by contrast, form the mythology of early childhood and the nursery-school years.[19]

How can the Story be linked with the stories and "myths" which can continue to serve as vehicles for communicating the message? Samuel Ijsseling writes:

> With the end of the grand narratives, the collapse of all ideologies…, sometimes the only possibility that remains is appealing to the age-old and fragmented stories, not so much to interpret them and seek a hidden message in them but to tell them anew, in a different place and at a different time, in a different context.[20]

But if one wishes to tell stories, what are the ones that serve as vehicles? One example that strikes me is the well-known novel by the US writer J.D. Salinger, *The Catcher in the Rye*. The main character is the 16-year-old Holden Caulfield. He is at the end of his rope, and runs away from home. Things have gone badly for him at school and in his relationships with his parents, friends and girlfriends. Finally, Holden ("Hold on"?) looks for his sister Phoebe during his ramblings about New York. Phoebe, whose name means "radiant" (one of Apollo's nicknames), actually wants nothing to do with him. But finally a conversation between the two begins, a conversation that is for me one of the most moving passages of the book.

> Then all of a sudden, she said, "Oh, why did you *do* it?" She meant why did I get the axe again. It made me sort of sad, the way she said it.
> "Oh, God, Phoebe, don't ask me. I'm sick of everybody asking me that," I said. "A million reasons why. It was one of the worst schools I ever went to. It was full of phonies. And mean guys. You never saw so many mean guys in your life. For instance, if you were having a bull session in somebody's room, and somebody wanted to come in, nobody'd let them in if they were some dopey, pimply guy. Everybody was always locking their door when somebody wanted to come in. And they had this goddam secret fraternity that I was too yellow not to join. There was this one pimply, boring guy, Robert Ackley, that wanted to get in. He kept trying to join, and they wouldn't let him. Just because he was boring and pimply. I don't even feel like talking about it. It was a stinking school. Take my word...
> "Even the couple of *nice* teachers on the faculty, they were phonies, too."[21]

Then his sister says something he does not understand:

> "What?" I said. "Take your mouth away. I can't hear you with your mouth that way."
> "You don't like *anything* that's happening."
> It made me even more depressed when she said that...
> "Name one thing."
> "One thing? One thing I like?" I said. "Okay."

Then he tells her the following story about a boy named James Castle:

> There was this one boy at Elkton Hills, named James Castle, that wouldn't take back something he said about this very

conceited boy, Phil Stabile. James Castle called him a very conceited guy, and one of Stabile's lousy friends went and squealed on him to Stabile. So Stabile, with about six other dirty bastards, went down to James Castle's room and went in and locked the goddam door and tried to make him take back what he said, but he wouldn't do it. So they started in on him. I won't even tell you what they did to him — it's too repulsive — but he *still* wouldn't take it back, old James Castle. And you should've seen him. He was a skinny little weak-looking guy, with wrists about as big as pencils. Finally, what he did, instead of taking back what he said, he jumped out the window. I was in the *shower* and all, and even I could hear him land outside. But I just thought something fell out the window, a radio or a desk or something, not a *boy* or anything. Then I heard everybody running through the corridor and down the stairs, so I put on my bathrobe and I ran downstairs too, and there was old James Castle laying right on the stone steps and all. He was dead, and his teeth, and blood, were all over the place, and nobody would even go near him. He had on this turtleneck sweater I'd lent him. All they did with the guys that were in the room with him was expel them. They didn't even go to jail.

Finally, Phoebe asks Holden what he would like to do with his life:

"You know what I'd like to be? I mean if I had my goddam choice?"

"What? Stop *swearing*."

"You know that song 'If a body catch a body comin' through the rye'? I'd like — "

"It's 'If a body *meet* a body comin' through the rye'!"...

"I thought it was 'If a body catch a body'," I said. "Anyway, I keep picturing all these little kids playing some game in this big field of rye and all. Thousands of little kids, and nobody's around — nobody big, I mean — except me. And I'm standing on the edge of some crazy cliff. What I have to do, I have to catch everybody if they start to go over the cliff — I mean if they're running and they don't look where they're going I have to come out from somewhere and *catch* them. That's all I'd do all day. I'd just be the catcher in the rye and all. I know it's crazy, but that's the only thing I'd really like to be. I know it's crazy."

This story reads like a poignant modern parable. In my view, it touches on the mystery of what the gospel is all about. This boy — who has lost all hold on his life, who is a victim himself, as young as he is, already battered by life and near enough the abyss to feel its suction — wants to be the helper of those who are in danger of falling into the abyss. Here is the mystery of the gospel, of Jesus who was himself a "wounded healer".

Word and image

How can the gospel be communicated in an age of cinema and television? It has been said that "the moving image of the film is not so much a de*piction* as an *image*ination, the locus of an infinite spectrum of new meanings". The Russian director Andrei Tarkovski (one of whose films deals with the great 15th-century iconographer Andrei Rublev) and the Polish film-maker Krystof Kieslowski have even been called "new prophets" whose films are the medium for the appearance of the holy. "The light of the Creator is reflected in their il*lumin*ation."[22]

In a recent book Sylvain de Bleeckere has drawn a fascinating parallel between Kieslowski's work and the last great novel of the Dutch writer Harry Mulisch, *De ontdekking van de hemel* ("The Discovery of Heaven"). What follows draws on de Bleeckere's analysis.[23]

In the epilogue of his novel Mulisch allows the inhabitants of heaven to speak. They are disillusioned. They are debating a report which has been published going into great detail about what the loss of the presence of heaven has led to on earth. The spokesperson for the heavenly Chief puts it this way:

> It is complete. The world has finished... except Lucifer ["the devil"]... The only thing that remained for us [the inhabitants of heaven] after more than three thousand years was to take

back the ten words [i.e., the ten commandments]. An impotent gesture, of course, like a cheated girl giving her engagement ring back. Cold comfort, symbolic act, melancholy farewell. The decalogue was the ultimate thing on earth: the Chief's contract with humanity, concluded with its agent, the Jewish people, represented by its leader Moses in the role of notary. From now on Lucifer has free rein...

Thus the pessimism of the inhabitants of heaven in Mulisch's novel has to do with the obligatory taking back of the ten commandments. In their eyes, the divine Code no longer has any effect. Only Lucifer still has influence (p.123).

Kieslowski's series of films *The Decalogue*, which have often been shown on European television, exemplify a modern Christian interpretation of the ten commandments. Together with a friend, Kieslowski wrote screenplays for ten short films of about an hour each which related in one way or another to the biblical ten commandments. The setting is primarily a cheerless district of contemporary Warsaw. Through the ten commandments, Kieslowski reflects on the contemporary crisis of values.

In several "episodes", including the first of the series, "The First Commandment" (p.124), Kieslowski refers to the power exercised by modern science. The first and great commandment reads: "Love God". In this film Kieslowski focusses on the problem of the human relation to God in a contemporary culture in which atheism and agnosticism have penetrated into everyone's daily life. The film centres on the relationship between Krysztof, a university lecturer in linguistics and lapsed Catholic, and his young son Pawel. Krysztof "has invested his whole faith in the power of scientific thinking, which makes his grip on things stronger, thanks to developments in computer science" (p.11).

"The First Commandment", whose text might fit on one sheet of ordinary typing paper, says a great deal through its images. Kieslowski shows what Krysztof actually represents by filming him, for example, during a lecture to his students and allowing him to be seen through the eyes of his son, thus making evident how "odd" a character he really is. "The domain of the truth is not that of pure understanding which marks its terrain on the blackboard. The truth comes to light in the intimate space of the living room where people try to deal with one another" (p.12). In his living room, in the face of his son's questions, the father stumbles on the limits of his atheistic theory: "Why do people die? Why does death exist? What remains after death?" These questions echo the sadness that the young boy felt after seeing a dead dog (p.13). But Pawel's aunt Irena, who cares for him with all the concern of a mother (his parents are divorced), does give him an answer: "Maybe a life like your father's seems more reasonable, but that does not mean there is no God. Also for your papa. Do you understand?" Pawel answers, "Not very well." Then she speaks about her faith: "God is there. That is very simple if you believe." Pawel asks if *she* believes, to which Irena answers, "Yes." The child continues: "Who is he?" At the beginning of their conversation his aunt had told Pawel that life is a gift. The greatest joy in life is to be able to do something that helps someone else. And now she answers the child's question about the existence of God not with a word or a theory but with an eloquent gesture. She takes him into her arms and asks him what he feels. He says, "I love you." To which she replies, "And that too is God" (p.14).

From his university chair Krysztof pronounces the ultimate word about the omnipotence of human knowledge. But Kieslowski offers a telling image of the professor's fundamental lack of power. He allows this to emerge through Krysztof's performance not in the university lecture-hall but on the little stage of everyday life.

It is there, according to Sylvain de Bleeckere, that one finds "the deep traces of the decalogue. Along that trail, in the modern world of Lucifer where no account is taken of the ten commandments, where heaven, where God has disappeared, arises a way that leads to the actual discovery of heaven." He goes on to say that although Harry Mulisch's novel appeared several years after Kieslowski's film, the *Decalogue* has gone beyond *De ontdekking van de hemel*. Kieslowski has discovered more of heaven on earth than Mulisch did.

> From their all-too-heavenly field of vision the inhabitants of heaven discover only the omnipresent influence of Lucifer. Their discoveries evidence an all-too-distant look at the human way of life on earth. With the aesthetic eye of the camera, the instrument with which Kieslowski sets up his story, more can be discovered: love. Perhaps the heavenly distance from which the intellectual inhabitants of heaven look at the world is the reason they are unable to see the *traces of light* in the darkness — traces of the presence of God (p.124).

One catches — in a secularized world where heaven seems to be undiscovered territory — something of *A Rumour of Angels*, to use the phrase of the US sociologist of religion Peter Berger (who had spoken earlier of the breakdown of "the sacred canopy").[24]

As to the question of how to translate the gospel in modern European culture, I would want to say that "the ABC of universal symbolism stands next to the biblical ABC". The Dutch theologian A.A. van Ruler has some important insights into this:

> The church, Christians and mission are never more than the little cart, the vehicle, on which the Word of God — the written, the canonical, the Israelite word — moves from one person to another, from one time to another, from one people to another. The Bible is again and again set down, and then we must — on principle — leave it to its own destiny, that is, to the Holy Spirit, and wait to see what happens with the Bible and what that other person, that other time, that other people do with the Bible... The Bible is fully the living witness of the Holy Spirit only when it resonates in the hearts and lives of persons. And there is not only the Bible, the Word of God, God himself — the human being is there as well, respected pneumatically in his or her freedom and independence. The person does something with God's own Word whenever he or

she makes it his or her own!... The intention that the Word of God is thus *changed into something unrecognizable* is also pneumatic. [25]

It follows from this last remark of van Ruler that in the translation of the gospel one can go quite far in showing respect for what human beings have said in their culture. One cannot fall back on a simple biblicism. One must chart a course between the Scylla of biblicism (whether fundamentalist or not) — conjuring with biblical texts treated as eternal truths (for example, "no other name", Acts 4:12, or "no other way", John 14:6) — and the Charybdis of a thoroughgoing syncretism — in the negative sense that is always given to it. The latter charge is too easily levelled in the usually prejudicial Western Christian approach to and assessment of the links made between gospel and culture in Africa and Asia.

The question of the authenticity or inauthenticity of European culture must continue to be posed. It is not the case that "anything goes". There are after all two forms of *Aufhebung*. The contact with our modern European culture must always be critical. Some myths must be combatted. The Dutch theologian K.H. Miskotte did that with his book *Edda en Thora*, written in 1939 in the context of the revival of Germanic paganism. Miskotte pointed out the dangers of syncretism — of what we might call today a wrong contextualization. But recognition of the ambivalence of every culture, including modern European and Western culture, should not prevent the church from continuing to seek out the possibilities of positive points of contact.

It is evident from the above that this is precisely what was done in Europe in the past, and there is no other way than that of contextualization. If the Celtic Christians saw the presence of God in the sun, the moon, the stars and the whole earth, that does not have to be called pantheism, as is often suggested. "For the Celt creation is translucent; it lets through glimpses of the glory of God," says Saunders Davies. [26] It is better in this case to speak of *panentheism* than of pantheism: seeing God as a being in all creation but also as having existence outside of it. The traditions of the Druids were not destroyed by Celtic Christianity but redeemed, transfigured and fulfilled. [27]

Like the church in the past, the church today has a unique message that it will continue to wish to pass on, which is not the same as what is encountered in specific cultures. What has been said regarding the connection of Christianity with Greek culture remains true:

> Greatness in the sense of humble service and a choice for the weak, poor and oppressed human, for the widow and orphan, did not fit into Greek culture... The Greeks had no room for a figure like Abraham, who is called the righteous person *par excellence*, or for someone like Francis of Assisi, who chose poverty, not to speak of the crucified Christ. [28]

Humility — a virtue that ranks high in Christian ethics — is something for which the ancient Greeks had little or no use. "The gospel opts for the small and the least, the children and the disparaged, those without opportunities who must be cared for." [29] The Greeks had no confidence in their gods. Their friendship had to be bought with sacrifices and the recognition by humans of their own finitude, but they were never to be trusted. [30] This of course is at odds with the fundamental biblical idea of God as eternally trustworthy, the God conceived as eternally loving humankind (cf. Titus 3:4), as Schillebeeckx puts it.

Examples drawn from the past can, I believe, also inspire us in an age when the visual culture has become so predominant to connect the Old Story with the visual stories of today. For the heart of the matter is still a "Story", a "Mystery", of "what no eye has seen, nor ear heard, nor the human heart conceived, what God has prepared for those who love him" (1 Cor. 2:9; cf. Isa. 64:4). Consider, for example, the success in recent years of the musical *Les Misérables*, based on Victor Hugo's well-known novel. What the public has been reacting to with enthusiasm and recognition night after night in several European countries is a work in which the basic themes are the very ones of the gospel: reconciliation, redemption, absolution and forgiveness.

The Dutch preacher and poet Jan Wit says in one of his songs: "It is all a parable of a mystery beyond this world." It is said that as a punishment for his unbelief the Irish saint Brendan (c. 484–577), the patron saint of sailors, had to wander around creation to observe God's miracles and to note them down. Jan Wit points, as the Celtic poets once did,[31] to the character of God's creation as sign:

> You have clothed the flowers of the fields
> With royal splendour.
> The carefree birds proclaim
> That you do not forget your creation.
> *It is all a parable*
> *Of a mystery beyond this world.*

It is fascinating that this blind poet points to the continuing need not only of hearing but also of seeing:

> Let my heart, then, belong to you
> And let me go through the world
> *with open eyes, open ears,*
> *To understand all your signs.*
> Then earthly life is good
> Because heaven greets me.

NOTES

[1] Emile Mâle, *De religieuze kunst van de XIIe tot de XVIIIe eeuw*, Utrecht and Brussels, 1949, pp.99ff. (italics added); cf. his "Medieval Iconography", in Harold Spencer, ed., *Readings in Art History*, New York, 1969, p.286.

[2] Abraham Kuyper, *E Voto Dordraceno: Toelichting op den Heidelbergschen Catechismus*, Kampen, n.d., Vol. 3, p.576.

[3] The phrase is from Jacques Ellul, *La parole humiliée*, Paris, 1981; Eng. tr., *The Humiliation of the Word*, Grand Rapids, 1985.

[4] Sylvain de Bleeckere, *Het licht van de schepping: de religiositeit van de beeldcultuur*, Helmond, 1992, p.23; on visual culture see also Jacques de Visscher and Kees Vuyk, *Kan een beeldcultuur zonder het woord?*, Kampen, 1994.

[5] N. Postman, *Amusing Ourselves to Death: Public Discourse in the Age of Show Business*, New York, 1987.

[6] Robert W. Brockway, *Myth from the Ice Age to Mickey Mouse*, pp. 136-44.

[7] Cf. John A. Coleman, "The Sociology of the Media", *Concilium*, VI, 1993, pp.3-11.

[8] Henk Hoekstra, "Audiovisuelle Sprache und Kultur: Moralische Bildung", in U.F. Schmälze, ed., *Neue Medien — Mehr Verantwortung: Analysen und pädagogischen Handreichungen zur ethischen Medienerziehung in Schule und Jugendarbeit*, Bonn, 1992, pp.76f.

[9] *Ibid.*, p.81.

[10] Gregory Baum, "The Church and the Mass Media", *Concilium*, VI, 1993, pp.63-70.

[11] Cited in *Nieuwe Rotterdamse Courant*, 2 June 1995.

[12] Baum, *loc. cit.*, p.63, citing the Vatican II Pastoral Constitution on the Church in the Modern World (*Gaudium et Spes*), para. 44.

[13] On these windows by Chagall, see Klaus Mayer, *St Stephan in Mainz*, Munich and Zurich, 1990.

[14] This is discussed in more detail in Wessels, *Europe: Was It Ever Really Christian?*, ch. 5; cf. W.C. Smith, *What Is Scripture? A Comparative Approach*, pp. 362ff.

[15] Roger Sherman Loomis, *Celtic Myth and Arthurian Romance*, London, 1993, p.39.

[16] J. Blauw, *Mens, kultuur en maatschappij: Lotgevallen van een denktraditie*, Nijkerk, 1978, pp.10.

[17] Quoted by Joseph Campbell, *The Flight of the Wild Gander: Mythological Dimensions of Fairy Tales, Legends and Symbols*, San Francisco, 1990; cf. Brockway, *op.cit.*, pp.11,95; R. Carter, *The Tao and Mother Goose*, Wheaton, Illinois, 1988.

[18] Campbell, *op. cit.*, p.6.

[19] Carter, *op. cit.*, pp.58f.

[20] S. Ijsseling, *Apollo, Dionysos, Aphrodite en de anderen: Griekse goden in de hedendagse filosofie*, Amsterdam, 1994, p.196.

[21] The passages cited here are from pp.167-73 in the edition published by Bantam Books, New York, in 1950.

[22] De Visscher and Vuyk, *op. cit.*, p.5.

[23] Harry Mulisch, *De ontdekking van de hemel*, Amsterdam, 1994, p.899; cited by Sylvain de Bleeckere, *Levenswaarden en levensverhalen: Een studie van de decaloog van Kieslowski*, Louvain and Amersfoort, 1994; other page references in this section are to this work by de Bleeckere.
[24] Peter Berger, *A Rumour of Angels: Modern Society and the Rediscovery of the Supernatural*, Garden City, NY, 1969; *The Sacred Canopy: Elements of a Sociological Theory of Religion*, Garden City, repr. 1990.
[25] A.A. van Ruler, *Theologie van het Apostolaat*, Nijkerk, pp. 24-25; italics added. I am grateful to Hans Abma for calling my attention to this passage.
[26] Quoted by Brockway, *op. cit.*, p.35.
[27] Anthony Duncan, *The Elements of Celtic Christianity*, p.68.
[28] Ijsseling, *op. cit.*, p.97.
[29] *Ibid.*, p.101.
[30] *Ibid.*, p.195.
[31] Cf. Esther de Waal, *The Celtic Vision: Prayers and Blessings from the Outer Hebrides*, London, 1988.